PROTECTING OUR PLANET

Energy in Crisis

Catherine Chambers

CRABTREE
Publishing Company
www.crabtreebooks.com

Crabtree Publishing Company
www.crabtreebooks.com

Author:
Catherine Chambers

Editorial director:
Kathy Middleton

Proofreaders:
Crystal Sikkens,
Molly Aloian

Designer:
Paul Myerscough

Production coordinator:
Kenneth Wright

Prepress technician:
Kenneth Wright

Illustrations:
Geoff Ward

Cover:
The way that energy is produced and the amount we use have a huge impact upon our planet. If we continue to use fuels at the current rate, the earth will run out of resources and the effects of polution will be devastating.

Photos:
Alamy Images: F1online digitale Bildagentur GmbH p. 4; Corbis: EPA/Adrian Bradshawp. 27, EPA/ Wu Hong p. 15b, Barbara Kraft p. 5; Fotolia: Sisu p. 15t; Getty Images: AFP/Stringer p. 12, AFP/Khin Maung Wins p. 16, Riser/John Lund p. 14; Istockphoto: Niels van Gijn p. 9t, James Steidlp. 24–25, Dale Taylor p. 24, Anantha Vardhan p. 19b; NASA: C. Mayhew & R. Simmon (NASA/GSFC), NOAA/NGDC, DMSP p. 9b; Photolibrary: Phototake Science/Richard Nelridge p. 10; Photoshot: NHPA/Manfred Danegger p. 7; Rex Features: Albanpix Ltd p. 25; Science Photo Library: Hank Morgan p. 26; Shutterstock: Ian Bracegirdle p. 1, 3, 30–31, 32, Pichugin Dmitry p. 6–7, Fouquin p. 18–19, Jarvis Gray p. 22–23, Joanne Harris and Daniel Bubnich p. 11b, iofoto p. 23t, Rafa Irusta p. 20–21, Falk Kienas p. 21, Morgan Lane Photography p. 28, David Mckee p. 8, Oleg Z p. 12–13, PhotoSmart p. 16–17, Mark William Richardson p. 10–11, Carolina K. Smith, M.D. p. 19t, Thomas Sztanek p. 4–5, WizData Inc p. 28–29, Hugo de Wolf 11t, Tania Zbrodko 26–27; Still Pictures: Biosphoto/Coupard Michel 23b.

Cover photograph:
Shutterstock (Renars Jurkovskis)

Library and Archives Canada Cataloguing in Publication

Chambers, Catherine, 1954-
    Energy in crisis / Catherine Chambers.

(Protecting our planet)
Includes index.
ISBN 978-0-7787-5212-7 (bound).--ISBN 978-0-7787-5229-5 (pbk.)

    1. Power resources--Juvenile literature. 2. Renewable energy
sources--Juvenile literature. I. Title. II. Series: Protecting our planet
(St. Catharines, Ont.)

TJ163.23.C43 2010   j333.79   C2009-905264-4

Library of Congress Cataloging-in-Publication Data

Chambers, Catherine, 1954-
    Energy in crisis / Catherine Chambers.
       p. cm. -- (Protecting our planet)
    Includes index.
    ISBN 978-0-7787-5229-5 (pbk. : alk. paper)
    -- ISBN 978-0-7787-5212-7 (reinforced lib. bdg. : alk. paper)
    1. Power resources--Juvenile literature. 2. Renewable energy
resources--Juvenile literature. I. Title. II. Series.

    TJ163.23.C44 2010
    333.79--dc22

                                                    2009034884

Crabtree Publishing Company

www.crabtreebooks.com   1-800-387-7650

Published in Canada
Crabtree Publishing
616 Welland Ave.
St. Catharines, ON
L2M 5V6
Printed in China/122009/CT20090915

Published in the United States
Crabtree Publishing
PMB16A
350 Fifth Ave., 59th floor
New York, NY 10118

Published by CRABTREE PUBLISHING COMPANY.
Copyright © **2010**

Contents

What is the energy crisis?

Energy makes things work. From coal and wood, to gas and oil, planet Earth has a wealth of natural resources packed full of energy. However, we are using these resources up so quickly that we are running out of them—and damaging the planet in the process. We are facing an energy crisis.

The amount of energy a person uses depends on their lifestyle, and where he or she lives. In India, for example, energy **consumption**, or use, has risen dramatically as people in parts of the country benefit from improved lifestyles.

Why should India reduce its energy consumption when over 400 million people in India do not even have access to regular electricity supplies? Also, the majority of people in Western Europe use vast amounts of electricity every day.

"The huge energy challenges facing China and India are global energy challenges and call for a global response."

Nobuo Tanaka, Executive Director of International Energy Agency, 2007

CASE STUDY

India

Today, in the noisy, bustling Indian city of Mumbai, formerly Bombay, cars and trucks jostle for space with rickshaws, bicycles, and cattle. Twenty years ago, there were only a few cars.

India is becoming richer as industries grow. Many more people in India have better lifestyles, with more money to spend on energy-guzzling items such as cars and fridges—items that others around the world have taken for granted for many years.

Over one billion people live in India. By 2050 the figure is expected to reach 1.6 billion, making India the world's most populated country. India's energy consumption will soar—it is expected to double by 2030.

India depends upon coal to produce nearly three-quarters of its electricity. Coal releases more harmful quantities of carbon dioxide gas into the atmosphere than any other way of generating energy. It is widely accepted that carbon dioxide **emissions** are responsible for **climate change**.

▲ *Businesses worldwide need a lot of energy. This conference center is powering over 100 laptops.*

Around the world, individuals and governments are concerned with the immediate dangers of climate change, such as rising sea levels. Countries, such as the United States—that have released the most carbon dioxide due to their consumption of **fossil fuels** such as coal and oil—want newly emerging countries such as India to reduce both their carbon dioxide emissions and energy consumption. The Indian government argues that its country is not responsible for the current energy crisis.

◄ *The streets of Mumbai, India, have become very polluted as a result of the huge increase in the number of cars, trucks, and buses.*

What is energy?

All life needs energy. Plants get energy from the Sun, while animals can get energy from the plants they eat. We, too, get energy from the food we eat. But since we discovered fire, we have taken extra energy from Earth to make life easier and more comfortable.

Sourcing energy

At the flick of a switch, electrical energy makes a light bulb glow. Turn on the gas and heat energy makes water boil. Energy comes in different forms such as light and heat.

Electrical energy comes from different fuels or sources. Heat energy from burning coal, oil, or gas can be turned into electrical energy.

▼ *Energy provided by electricity plants powers modern civilization. It allows us to cook food, watch television, and light our homes.*

> "Global energy needs are expected to grow with fossil fuels remaining the dominant source, sharply pushing up CO_2 (carbon dioxide) emissions with dramatic implications for all countries . . . Vigorous and immediate policy responses are needed to set us on a more sustainable energy path."
>
> **World Energy Outlook, 2007**

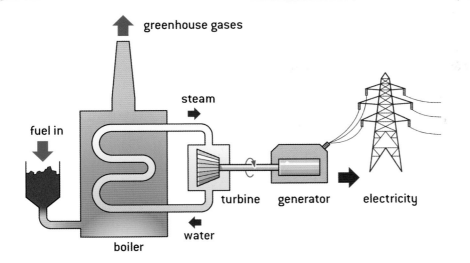

greenhouse gases

steam

fuel in

turbine generator electricity

water

boiler

Energy can be generated by heating water. A boiler burns fuel and turns water to steam. The steam turns a turbine, which spins a generator. This action produces electricity.

Renewable and non-renewable

Some fuels, such as wood from trees, or energy in the form of heat from the Sun, or the force from the wind, are **renewable**. Trees can grow again and the Sun and the wind are always present. Other fuels, such as coal, oil, and natural gas are **non-renewable**. They are formed over millions of years, but they will not form again for millions more years. This means that once they are used they will not be available again.

What's the problem?

The way that energy is produced and the amount we use have a huge impact upon Earth. If we continue to use fuels at the current rate, Earth will run out of its own resources. The climate will be thrown into further chaos and future generations will suffer. The effect on the **environment** will be devastating—this way of living is **unsustainable**.

WHAT CAN BE DONE?

Energy consumption can be reduced. Saving energy reduces the need to burn fuels. This preserves existing fuel resources and does not add to harmful carbon dioxide levels. Using alternative renewable energy, such as solar power, also helps the environment. Less polluting fuel sources offer a **sustainable** solution to the crisis.

A kestrel eats mice to give it energy. People need energy from food and fuels to be able to lead their lives.

Burning it up

If everyone on Earth burned up energy at the current levels used in the United States, we would need the resources of five more similar planets. At the rate energy is used in Bangladesh, people would need just a third of Earth's resources.

Needing more and more

As the first trains took to the tracks, coal-mining became a key industry because coal supplied the steam to power the trains. The invention of the electric light increased demand for electricity supplies. As cars became more popular, the demand for oil, that can be converted into gas, soared. Today, oil is used to make plastics, chemicals, and many everyday materials.

Energy matters

Hospital equipment runs on electricity. Schools need warmth and light in buildings so children can learn. At home, people enjoy hot water, cooked food, and warmth for normal health needs. All of these everyday things depend on reliable energy sources. However, there are two billion people in the world without access to electricity.

This Bangladeshi ferry ▶
man's energy needs
are a fraction of those
of a Westerner.

When the cost of the coal, oil, or natural gas rises, so too does a trip to the seaside, or even the cost of a loaf of bread. The price of oil has recently shot upwards. For some people, this is an inconvenience and means cutting back a little on their spending. For others, it means being unable to afford to buy rice to feed their family.

We take electrical power for granted and only realize how much we depend upon it when there is a power failure. On a blisteringly hot day in 2003, cities across the east coast of North America ground to a halt. A massive power failure of the electricity supply switched off electrically powered machines over a distance of more than 2,786 miles (4,484 km). From traffic lights to air-conditioning systems, everything electrical ceased to work for over 12 hours. Over 50 million people were

▲ *Many people in Bangladesh live in great poverty. They are without clean water or electricity supplies.*

affected, and some people were trapped in subway trains and lifts. The blackout may have been because of a breakdown in an electrical transmission line combined with exceptionally high electrical usage from air-conditioning on a hot, humid day.

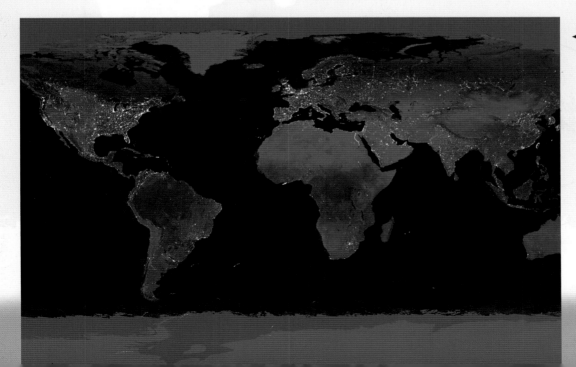

◄ *The lights in this satellite picture show where the most energy is being used on Earth.*

9

Fossil fuels

Most of the energy that we use comes from burning fossil fuels. These fuels, such as coal, oil, and gas, formed from the remains of dead animals and plants. Over millions of years, the dead matter sank deep underground or to the bottom of the sea, buried under layers of other plants.

Getting hotter

Burning fossil fuels, especially coal, in power stations releases large amounts of a gas called carbon dioxide, or CO_2. Too much carbon dioxide in Earth's atmosphere is the main cause of **global warming**, the worldwide increase in temperature which is driving climate change. Warmer temperatures play havoc with Earth's weather and **ecosystems**. Animals, crops, and humans are struggling to cope with the changing conditions. The burning of fossil fuels is the main cause of climate change.

▲ *Most coal is locked underground and we need to dig it up to use it.*

Running out

Oil and natural gas supplies will run out this century—at current rates, perhaps in 40 or 60 years. New oil and gas fields are being discovered and drilled, but these, too, will run out. There is enough coal to last for over 100 more years, but coal is the most polluting fossil fuel.

Kyoto Protocol

Scientists and politicians agree that it is necessary to reduce carbon dioxide emissions. In 1997, the Kyoto Protocol, an international agreement, set a maximum amount of carbon dioxide emissions that more economically developed countries could produce.

This came into force in 2005. China still refuses to sign the agreement.

▲ *Oil refineries take black, sticky oil and turn it into gas and other products.*

▲ *Planting a tree is a positive action that can be done by everyone.*

WHAT CAN BE DONE?

Some people donate money to plant trees when they take a long flight, because a tree will absorb carbon dioxide gas. This way of offsetting carbon dioxide emissions is often described as making a journey "carbon neutral." But it may take over 20 years for a growing tree to absorb all the carbon produced by a single flight. If this is not strictly a sustainable solution, we need to find fuels that do not release so many harmful gases. Perhaps we should change our habits and fly less frequently.

11

Wood fires

From pine to palm, trees are habitats for animals and insects. Trees stabilize the soil with their roots and help keep the air healthy. It is easy to chop down trees for wood, which burns well. When trees are replanted to replace those that have been chopped down, the wood is seen as a renewable energy source.

Lungs of the world

Without Earth's covering of towering trees, the levels of carbon dioxide would be even greater. As a tree converts energy from the Sun it absorbs carbon dioxide. The carbon is stored in the tree's trunk, branches, and leaves. The tree then releases oxygen back into the atmosphere. Burning wood releases carbon dioxide into the atmosphere, but tree cover helps to absorb it, as it maintains a healthy balance of gases.

◄ *In many parts of the world, wood is a very important resource. These Indian tribeswomen collect it for heating and cooking.*

12

Chopped down

Forests are cleared for land to grow crops for **biofuels**. Many industries use charcoal from wood to produce electricity. People are cutting down huge areas of forests for the fuel. **Deforestation** alters the strength and **fertility** of the soil. Without trees' roots to absorb rainfall, soil washes away in heavy rains, causing soil **erosion**. As rain washes away, the soil becomes weak and dry. The spread of dusty land, called **desertification**, leads to less fertile land on which crops can grow.

CASE STUDY

Kwimba Reforestation Project, Tanzania

Near Lake Victoria in Tanzania, local people farm, growing crops and keeping cattle and goats. Children and women used to spend hours walking to collect bundles of firewood for fuel. As more trees were cut down, people had to walk even further to find fuel. Soon, the area had lost most of its natural tree cover. A reforestation project began in the early 1990s. Millions of fast-growing trees were planted. Now the local women and children can again find firewood nearby. The land is fertile once more for crop-growing. This project has provided an immediate answer to the community's energy needs. It has maintained the area's **ecological** balance and **bio-diversity**, while it also provides healthy land for future generations—this is a sustainable answer to an energy problem.

▲ *Sustainable solutions help the environment. If forests are cut down, they need to be replanted.*

Polluted air

Gray clouds of soot and smoke billow out from factory chimneys. Often the **particles**, or bits, of pollution in the air are invisible, but they can be every bit as dangerous as visible smoke and soot. Small pieces of soot can cause breathing difficulties and even fatal illnesses.

Smoky wood

Breathing in too much wood smoke damages a person's health as particles from the burnt wood become trapped in their lungs. This is a problem for families in poorer parts of the world, where wood is the main source of fuel inside the home. Wood is often burned without a stove to channel away the smoke. Estimates suggest that this type of indoor air pollution causes the death of 1.6 million people every year—or the equivalent of one person dying every 20 seconds.

Raining acid

Fumes from cars and factories also contain gases such as sulphur dioxide and nitrogen oxides. These **pollutants** mix with water vapor—water as an invisible gas—in the air and fall back to the ground in rain. This is known as acid rain, because it eats away at trees and even stone statues.

◄ *Wood is used as a fuel inside homes in Vietnam. The smoke is a health hazard.*

Acid rain can harm trees, as well
as fish and fresh water supplies.

CASE STUDY

China

People in Chinese cities are wearing masks in warm weather. Athletes avoid running or doing vigorous exercise outside. This is China, a country with a booming industry and economy. The air pollution in China is caused by the massive increase in energy consumption. China builds about one coal-burning power plant each week. Gases from the coal-fired power plants fall back to the land as acid rain. In some cities, people wear masks to protect themselves from the toxic cocktail of air pollution from ash, soot, diesel exhaust, and chemicals. At least 400,000 Chinese citizens die each year from diseases related to air pollution.

Linfen in China is one of the most
polluted cities on Earth. Many
people wear breathing masks.

15

Climate chaos

The increased rate of climate change in recent years has brought about more flooding and droughts—destroying crops and leading to food shortages. Droughts cause water shortages. Warmer temperatures destroy ecosystems and habitats on land and at sea. This climate crisis is caused by the human use of fuels.

A question of balance

A certain amount of carbon dioxide high in the atmosphere naturally keeps Earth's temperature in balance. But too much carbon dioxide traps too much heat like a hot greenhouse, causing global warming. Carbon dioxide levels have risen as we burn more fossil fuels.

Extreme weather

Hurricane Katrina ravaged parts of New Orleans in the United States in 2005. The devastating Cyclone Nargis battered the country of Myanmar, formerly known as Burma, in 2008, killing thousands of people. Such extreme weather events are becoming more frequent and fiercer.

Scientists believe that there is a link between the pollution caused by burning fossil fuels and the frequency and strength of such extreme weather events.

Warmer seas

Sea levels are rising because warmer temperatures, caused by global warming, are melting ice caps in the freezing polar regions. Warmer seawater takes up more space than cold waters.

Cyclone Nargis killed an ➤
estimated 130,000 people
in Myanmar in 2008.

As sea levels rise, low-lying coastal areas in countries such as Bangladesh and the Netherlands could be swamped by water. The change in temperature affects delicately balanced ecosystems as animals try to adapt to the changing conditions. In the seas, mighty whales suffer. Tiny animals called krill cannot survive in warm waters. Without krill to eat, their predators go hungry. Without the krills' predators to feast upon, or the krill themselves, there is no food for the whale.

▼ *Half the world's hungry are small farmers. Many lose their entire crops to regular devastating droughts.*

> *". . . the emission of greenhouse gases associated with industrialization and economic growth from a world population that has increased sixfold in 200 years, is causing global warming at a rate that is unsustainable."*

Tony Blair, former UK prime minister, 2006

Fact bank

By the end of the century, with continued rises in **greenhouse gases** the likely effects may be:

- global temperature rise between 35° Fahrenheit (1.8°C) and 39° Fahrenheit (4°C).
- sea level to rise by 11–17 inches (28–43 cm).
- Arctic summer sea ice will disappear.
- increase in heatwaves worldwide.
- increase in tropical storm intensity.

What is biomass?

From cow dung to chip fat, waste can provide us with energy. Biomass is fuel that comes from plants or plant and animal waste. Burning biomass releases its stores of the Sun's energy. Is using waste the path toward a sustainable future?

Give and take

Biomass releases some carbon dioxide when burned. However, the animal or plant from which the biomass comes absorbs an equal amount of carbon dioxide during its lifetime. Burning fossil fuels releases carbon dioxide that plants and animals locked up millions of years ago, whereas burning biomass releases carbon dioxide locked up this year.

▼ *Biomass crops like the corn below can be used for fuel. But should the land be used to grow crops for food instead?*

> "I have four cows so I get good gas, so I do not need to collect firewood. I save a lot of time not collecting the wood and not washing soot from the pans and in cooking. I can spend more time on my own farm and working for other people."

Mrs. Munithayamamma from Siradhanahalli village, India

Biogas

Letting waste and dung decompose in a special tank produces gases. The biogas released can be used as a fuel. Biogas supplies cooking gas to thousands of families in the rural areas in India. Once the gas has been produced, any leftover waste matter fertilizes the soil to help healthy crops grow.

▲ *Biofuels are available at some fuel stations as an alternative to diesel.*

Biofuels

Across the world, fields sway with crops of corn, sugarcane, and rapeseed. These crops are not used as food but as fuel. As they grow, the crops use up carbon dioxide. Then the crops are turned into fuel, which releases this carbon dioxide back into the atmosphere as it burns.

▼ *Indian farmers can obtain methane gas from their cattle as a source of energy.*

WHAT CAN BE DONE?

In recent years, growing crops to be made into biofuels was a response to urgent concerns about the effect of fossil fuels on our planet and the need to find renewable, clean energy sources. However, there is evidence that growing biofuels on land once used to grow food has now contributed to severe food shortages and pushed up food prices around the world. Many people believe that we should stop growing biofuel crops on land that should be used for food crops.

Energy from weather

Can the Sun and wind provide a sustainable solution to the current energy crisis? The wind will not stop blowing and the Sun will not stop shining. Harnessing the power of these natural forces provides renewable energy.

As long as there are regular winds and sunny days, many countries can benefit from solar or wind power. Nearly 40 percent of Portugal's energy comes from solar, wind, and wave power. In poorer countries, in areas where there are no power stations and no networks of gas or oil pipes, solar power is often the only source of energy for cooking, heating, and lighting.

Hot light

A house built with a lot of windows naturally traps the Sun's heat. Special mirrors can also collect the Sun's heat and light to produce electricity. It is now possible to store the Sun's energy by trapping heat from the Sun in tanks or towers, rather like the way heat is stored in a thermos flask, so that there is still power on a cloudy day.

Wind turbines have tall ➤ towers because stronger winds blow higher off the ground.

Sunlit cells

Solar cells called photovoltaic cells convert the Sun's light into small stores of electricity like batteries. The process of producing photovoltaic cells uses up large amounts of energy from fossil fuels. It also involves some dangerous chemicals and is extremely expensive. Scientists are currently developing new techniques to improve the efficiency of solar cell production.

▼ *In South America, a reflective dish can be used to focus the Sun's rays. This generates enough heat to boil a kettle.*

Windy days

If you go for a walk in the countryside you may see rows of blades whizzing around on the top of tall poles. These are wind turbines. The wind turns the blades which spin a shaft. A **generator** converts this spinning energy into electrical energy. The energy produced does not cause pollution, and it is renewable. However, building wind turbines uses up a lot of concrete, a material that requires large amounts of energy to make. Many people have concerns that wind turbines spoil the landscape and make too much noise. There are reports, too, of birds being killed by the turning blades.

Natural power

From smoking volcanoes to wild waves, there is energy in Earth that can be converted into energy that powers a computer or heats a house.

Hot Earth

Hot springs or hot rock deep in Earth's core bubbles and boils. This heat from Earth, called **geothermal**, can be channeled to provide direct heat or can be converted into electrical energy.

Water power

People build dams across rivers to hold back swirling masses of water. When the water is finally released, the force of the gushing water is used to power a generator. This is hydropower. However, this "clean energy" source is not always good for the environment. Hydropower provides large amounts of electricity for thousands of local communities, but building the dams involves disruption to the land and to people living nearby. Dams alter a river's flow, changing

▲ *Scientists continue to experiment with ways of using the power of waves.*

▲ Hoover Dam, near Las Vegas in the United States, supplies power to about 14 million people.

Fact bank

- About 20 percent of electricity worldwide is generated by hydropower.

- Hydropower provides about: ten percent of the electricity in the United States, 99 percent of the electricity in Norway, and 75 percent of the electricity in New Zealand.

and even destroying the habitats of river animals. Salmon populations have been reduced along many dammed rivers because they cannot complete the journey from sea to river, during which they breed. In some rivers, "ladders" are built to help salmon bypass the dam. Underwater flashing lights help direct the night-time traveling American shad fish and allow them to navigate safely around turbines in the Susquehanna River in Pennsylvania, United States.

Moon power

The pull of the moon controls the ebb and flow of tides. Volumes of water flow inland and then fall back twice a day. This tidal movement can be converted into usable energy. In France, a tidal power scheme provides electricity for four percent of the surrounding region. But plans to build a large tidal power plant in Britain across the River Severn are in dispute. Environmentalists argue that the long-term effect upon ecosystems and biodiversity will be drastic. Others argue that the energy supplied is renewable and will benefit the environment as it will not release any carbon gases.

▼ This tidal power plant near St. Malo, France, has used turbines to make energy since 1966.

23

Nuclear power

The fuel needed for nuclear power is a radioactive silver-gray metal called uranium. While France produces over two-thirds of its electricity from nuclear power, other countries will not even consider using it.

Making nuclear energy

From air to water, everything is made from atoms. The center of an atom, called a nucleus, contains electrons and neutrons. When a neutron splits a nucleus it releases vast amounts of energy. The atoms in uranium split easily. Uranium gives off invisible rays called radiation. These rays are extremely harmful in the concentrations used in nuclear power. Workers in nuclear power stations are covered from head to toe in protective clothing. Despite strict safety procedures at nuclear power plants, there have been serious accidents which have claimed many lives and caused serious illness.

▲ *In nuclear plants, two pounds (1 kg) of uranium produces as much energy as 3,000 tons (3,000 tonnes) of coal.*

Nuclear power creates more controversy than any other energy source that is an alternative to fossil fuels.

Deadly waste

The waste material produced in the making of nuclear power is deadly. No one has yet found a way to dispose of it safely. Today, nuclear waste is cooled in water for several years and then mixed into liquid glass, which is poured into steel containers. These containers are stored in a concrete-lined building. The material remains radioactive, or full of dangerous radiation, for hundreds of thousands of years.

Power for electricity or terror?

When uranium is used to make nuclear energy, it produces a very poisonous material called plutonium. This lethal material can be used to make nuclear weapons which can kill thousands of people in seconds. Nuclear power plants operate strict security procedures to prevent terrorists getting hold of this dangerous material.

WHAT CAN BE DONE?

Some people believe that nuclear power is the most efficient and clean alternative to fossil fuels. It is reliable and produces large quantities of energy. Others argue that mining for uranium destroys ecosystems and can release poisons into rivers and the soil. Uranium is dangerous and no one has found a way to get rid of its waste safely. Is nuclear power the answer to our energy crisis? Or are we making a poisonous time bomb of nuclear waste for future generations?

Future fuels?

The population of the world is set to rise by 3 billion in about 40 years. The International Energy Agency predicts a rise in global energy demand of 50–60 percent by 2030. How can we safeguard Earth's future while making sure everyone has enough energy?

Searching and testing

Scientists race to find new, clean energy sources. In Hawaii, tests are underway to turn the green, slimy stuff on ponds, tiny plants called algae, into biodiesel. Elsewhere, scientists are investigating if tiny organisms called microbes could be used to release trillions of tons (tonnes) of oil which is locked deep under the sea. Even if this is successful, oil is a fossil fuel that releases massive amounts of carbon dioxide when burned.

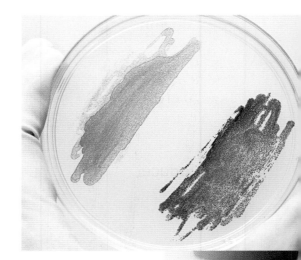

▲ Research is being carried out in laboratories in Hawaii to use algae as a form of biofuel.

"Climate change is our opportunity to advance sustainable development [and to]. . . encourage new kinds of cleaner technologies. . . "

United Nations Secretary-General Ban Ki-moon, 2008

The current use of gas and diesel fuel to run cars has become unsustainable. ➤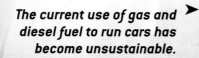

Cars from thin air

An Indian car manufacturer is working to deal with the energy crisis in India by developing an air-powered car. This car is powered by compressed, or squashed, air stored in special tanks. However, compressing the air uses up large amounts of energy. Another energy possibility is that cars may run on the very gas that people are trying to get rid of—carbon dioxide. Engineers are looking at ways to extract carbon from the air and convert it into a fuel.

Fuel cells

Fuel cells create electricity by mixing the gases hydrogen and oxygen. The only waste produced is water. However, electricity is required to produce hydrogen gas in the first place—and electricity is usually generated by burning fossil fuels. Scientists need to find an alternative fuel to create the hydrogen in order to make this a sustainable option for the future.

WHAT CAN BE DONE?

Solving energy problems is a global responsibility that demands action by all countries. This involves reducing the amount of carbon dioxide emissions but it also involves finding new, clean fuels for a sustainable future.

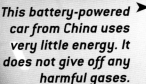

This battery-powered car from China uses very little energy. It does not give off any harmful gases. ➤

Protecting our planet

Governments and world leaders can make commitments about what their countries will do to provide energy sources that protect the planet. But what can we, as individuals, do?

> "Our earth is ailing. In its own language, it tells us that we must act together. . . to help it heal."
>
> **King Hussein of Jordan at the Earth Summit, 1992**

Fact bank

- One recycled tin can (instead of making a new one) would save enough energy to power a television for three hours.

- One recycled glass bottle would save enough energy to power a computer for 25 minutes.

- One recycled plastic bottle would save enough energy to power a 60-watt light bulb for three hours.

- Seventy percent less energy is required to recycle paper compared to making it from raw materials.

◄ We can all do our part to protect our planet. Recycling, as well as using less, helps.

HOW CAN WE PROTECT OUR PLANET?

- Work out, and try to reduce, your **carbon footprint**—this is the amount of greenhouse gas emissions you produce in your everyday life. There are several sites on the internet which help work out a carbon footprint.

- Recycle: using recycled material consumes less energy than using new materials.

- Reuse: buy products that can be used again. You will also save the energy used to make them, and reduce the amount of space needed to contain the waste. The land used for waste materials is known as landfill.

- Reduce: only buy what you need. This means that there will be less to throw away.

- Turn off lights or computers when they are not in use.

- Ride a bike or catch a bus or take a train instead of using a car. If you have to use a car to get to school, talk to your parents and try to share rides with friends who live nearby.

- Start a campaign at school to save energy.

- Ask your school to investigate using solar power or wind power, depending on where you live.

- Grow your own. Plant some vegetable seeds in a pot. Eating your own or locally produced food saves on energy spent sending food around the world to the supermarket.

- Compost your waste: buy a compost bin or worm composter to recycle your waste food scraps into compost. The compost you generate is ideal for growing new food or flowers.

The more we are able to recycle, the less space we use for landfill. ➤

Glossary

biodiversity   Range of life

biofuel   Fuel made from plants, or plant oils and animal wastes

carbon footprint   The amount of greenhouse gas emissions caused by an individual, organization, or product

climate change   Long-term changes in Earth's weather patterns

consumption   Use

deforestation   Chopping down huge areas of forest

desertification   The spread of dry and infertile land

ecological   To do with the relationship between living things and their environment

ecosystem   The balance between a community of animals and plants and its environment

emissions   Gases or chemicals released into the atmosphere

energy   Power from different fuels that makes things work

environment   The surroundings of plants, animals, and humans

erosion   The wearing away of land

fertility   The natural richness of land

fossil fuels   Fuels such as oil, coal, and gas. These fuels formed from the remains of plants and animals

geothermal   Using Earth's inner heat

generator   A machine used to make energy from various sources

global warming   The gradual warming of Earth's climate

greenhouse gases   Gases such as carbon dioxide which trap the Sun's heat around Earth

non-renewable   Resources that will not naturally form again for thousands of years

particles   Tiny pieces

pollutants   Gases and chemicals which cause pollution

renewable   Resources which will naturally form again in a short period of time

sustainable   Managing resources in a way that protects the environment and the resource

unsustainable   Using up resources too quickly so that they will not be available in the future

Further information

Books

What is the Future of Fossil Fuels? (Energy Revolution) by Ellen Rodger (Crabtree, 2010)

Fossil Power (Energy Sources) by Neil Morris (Franklin Watts, 2008)

Energy (Sustainable World) by Rob Bowden (Wayland, 2007)

Running out of Energy (Can the Earth Cope?) by Ewen McLeish (Wayland, 2007)

Saving Energy (Improving Our Environment) by Jen Green (Wayland, 2007)

Energy Supplies (Action for the Environment) by Chris Oxlade (Franklin Watts, 2006)

Web sites

Find out more about energy and how we use it at:
www.eia.doe.gov/kids/energyfacts/uses/manufacture.html

Get the facts on energy and take an energy quiz at this Web site:
www.ecokids.ca/pub/eco_info/topics/energy/ecostats/index.cfm

Find out what sustainability is all about and how to save energy:
www.olliesworld.com/planet/usa/info/issue/energy.htm

Calculate your own carbon footprint at:
www.mycarbonfootprint.eu/index.cfm?language=en

Index